A **FALCON** GUIDE®

Hiking with Dogs

BECOMING A WILDERNESS-WISE DOG OWNER

SECOND EDITION

Linda B. Mullally

Happy Trails !

Wouter

May 2007.

FALCON GUIDE®

GUILFORD, CONNECTICUT
HELENA, MONTANA

AN IMPRINT OF THE GLOBE PEQUOT PRESS

In memory of Lobo and Shiloh,
my beloved companions and teachers on the trail

*A*FALCONGUIDE®

Illustrations by Todd Telander and Diane Blasius
Design by Nancy Freeborn

Library of Congress Cataloging-in-Publication Data
Mullally, Linda B.
    Hiking with dogs: becoming a wilderness-wise dog owner / Linda B. Mullally.
    —2nd ed.
    p. cm. — (A FalconGuide)
    Includes bibliographical references (p. 87)
    ISBN-13: 978-0-7627-4011-6
    ISBN-10: 0-7627-4011-6
    1. Hiking with dogs. I. Title

SF427.51.M85 2006
796.51—dc22   2006048975

Manufactured in the United States of America
Second Edition/First Printing

Contents

Acknowledgments, iv
Preface, vi

CHAPTER ONE **Why Hike with Your Dog?** 1

CHAPTER TWO **Choosing a Dog for the Trail,** 3

CHAPTER THREE **Bonding,** 15

CHAPTER FOUR **Obedience,** 18

CHAPTER FIVE **Training Tips and Tools,** 23

CHAPTER SIX **Conditioning Your Dog,** 30

CHAPTER SEVEN **Day Hike Gear,** 38

CHAPTER EIGHT **Backpacking Gear,** 49

CHAPTER NINE **On the Trail,** 54

CHAPTER TEN **Wildlife Conflicts,** 63

CHAPTER ELEVEN **Medical Emergencies and Treatment,** 71

CHAPTER TWELVE **Trail Etiquette,** 75

CHAPTER THIRTEEN **Hiking on Public Lands,** 79

APPENDIX A **Checklists,** 82

APPENDIX B **Sources for Dog Hiking Gear and Accessories,** 86

APPENDIX C **Recommended Reading and Resources,** 87

About the Author, 89

Acknowledgments

My love of hiking with my dog began in childhood between the banks of the St. Maurice and St. Lawrence Rivers in Trois-Rivieres, Quebec. On weekends I would leave the house at dawn with my best friend, Sophie, a grey miniature poodle, and we would disappear for hours to explore the wooded shores of the St. Maurice River.

Since then I have hiked thousands of miles of trails around the globe. My peak experiences are encased in every nature walk and backpacking trip shared with my two dogs, Lobo and Shiloh, during the sixteen short years we had together. I am forever indebted to them for enhancing my love affair with hiking and nature and for inspiring this book.

I also want to acknowledge the following people for their valuable contribution to this project:

My husband, David (who never had a dog as a child), for opening his mind and heart to the adventure of loving and living with Lobo and Shiloh, and for convincing me I had something important to share with other dog owners; my parents and brothers, for their continual support of my passion for dogs and my compassion for the environment; Henri Boudreau, the English composition teacher who first put the pen in my hand and nurtured my love for the written word; George Bishop, DVM, for his sound professional advice and patience for my endless questions; the team of workers and policymakers at dog-friendly Garland Ranch Regional Park in Carmel Valley, California, for providing Lobo, Shiloh, and hundreds of other dogs with several thousand acres of hiking trails to safely romp and sniff during their rambunctious puppyhood and spirited adulthood.

Thank you to my friend Molly Attell for the tales of humorous co-misery and ebullient moments we shared raising our primitive dogs.

A special thanks to park ranger Robert Chapin; Susie Bluford, dog trainer and breeder; Pat Tucker, wildlife biologist and cofounder of Wild Sentry Ambassador Wolf Program, for their time and expertise.

I am grateful to all the National Park and Forest Service personnel in Washington, D.C., who eagerly directed me through the maze of departments in my search for useful resources for dog owners.

Preface

The difference between walking and hiking isn't distance, but rather the surface of the path traveled and where it leads you. Whether you leash your dog for a short stroll or an all-day excursion, once you leave the pavement for the dirt trails that will bring you closer to nature, you and your dog are hiking.

Urban pressures recede as you take in lungfuls of fresh air, revel in scenic open spaces, and delight in your dog's exuberance in the natural world. Hiking can be fun, healthy, and enriching for any dog owner and his dog. Using my lifelong experiences as a dog owner and hiker and others' expert knowledge, in this book I will share with you information that will help make hiking with your dog a fun and safe activity.

This book is written to introduce the novice hiker/dog owner to the basics of hiking with his or her dog with step-by-step guidance and preparation, from the whelping box to the trail. It reinforces some basic principles while introducing new perspectives and useful tips intended to enhance the outdoor partnership between all hikers and their dogs.

CHAPTER ONE

Why Hike with Your Dog?

Hiking is a healthy, non-competitive, and inexpensive form of outdoor recreation. As a dog owner you have the privilege of having a live-in hiking companion who will enhance the experience in a way no other best friend can. Your dog's innate curiosity will make you notice and appreciate more of the natural world around you. His alertness and intuition can give you an added sense of security.

Hiking also provides time for quality bonding between owner and dog. And dog owners with busy schedules find that hiking is a convenient opportunity to combine their own and their dog's need for exercise and play in a safe, natural setting.

Hiking can be very beneficial to your dog physically and mentally. In addition to the opportunity for physical exercise, the natural smells, sights, and sounds off the beaten track are invigorating and rejuvenating. Hiking and the training regimen to keep your dog in good form can be excellent prevention for several physical and behavioral disorders and in some cases may help reduce the symptoms of other ailments.

According to statistics, one in three dogs in America is overweight, which is usually a result of feeding too much (often the wrong foods) and moving too little. As in humans, obesity can trigger more serious health problems including heart attack, high blood pressure, diabetes, or even arthritis. To determine how fit your dog is, use this simple rule: You should be able to feel your dog's ribs when you run your hands along her sides (*feel* them, not see them).

The stress on the joints from carrying the extra weight can also exacerbate preexisting conditions such as hip dysplasia. The exercise from hiking can help keep your dog trimmer and strengthen muscles that support the hips.

Hiking can also help dogs that suffer from boredom that can result in depressive lethargy or destructive behaviors. Regular exercise in the great outdoors can help mellow out high-strung dogs and dogs prone to overt dominance and aggression.

Hiking is a natural and enjoyable way for people and dogs to stay fit. Running up a dirt trail, leaping over streams, climbing on boulders, negotiating fallen limbs in the forest, and paddling circles in the lake keep a dog's spirit soaring and her body agile, trim, and toned.

CHAPTER TWO

Choosing a Dog for the Trail

The domestic dog has been traced back to the wolf, which roamed throughout North America, Europe, Asia, and India 12,000 years ago or more. Capitalizing on the dog's ancestral instinct to hunt and bond with his pack, people have been selectively breeding dogs to perform specialized functions for centuries. There are now more than 400 breeds of dogs recognized around the world, varying in size, appearance, and abilities. From the largest (Irish wolfhound) to the smallest (Chihuahua), all retain a somewhat instinctive link to their wild roots.

Hiking Potential by Breed

Although dogs should be evaluated on their individual merits, having an idea of what the dog (purebred or mixed breed) was originally bred to do helps you adjust your expectations about hiking potential. Breed history and characteristics will influence physical performance and how the dog's instincts will play out on the trail. Following is an overview of seven breed groups highlighting hiking compatibility and incompatibility.

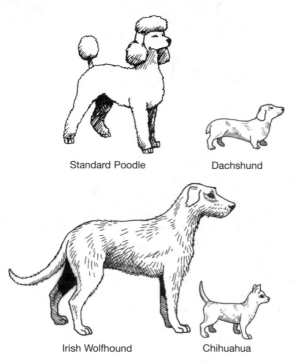

Standard Poodle

Dachshund

Irish Wolfhound

Chihuahua

All dogs, regardless of size or breed, retain a link to their wild roots.

Primitive Dog Breeds

This small group of natural dogs is believed to have its origin with the Asian wolf. Dogs with "primitive" stock are often defined by how minimally selective breeding has interfered with their natural legacy: medium size and balanced proportions for enduring swiftness on the hunt, prick eared, pointed muzzles, short- to medium-length coats, alert and aloof.

Breed examples: basenji, New Guinea singing dog, Australian cattle dog. Dingoes and New Guinea singing dogs are examples of primitive breeds at a very early stage of domestication.

Positive hiking traits: good stamina, agile, alert.

Concerns: Slow maturing, requiring more intense bonding and more time to respond to obedience training; strong hunting instincts that require patient, continuous reinforcement of impulse-control training, or life at the end of a leash to prevent chasing wildlife.

Sight and Scent Hounds
Bred to detect and track prey by superior sight and scent. Sight hounds are now being bred more for companionship than hunting.

Breed examples: greyhound, whippet, Afghan (sight hounds); bloodhound, basset hound, beagle (scent hounds).

Positive hiking traits: thrive on physical activity.

Concerns: Sight hounds instinctively want to chase small animals, including small dogs. Chasing all that moves is of particular concern with retired race dogs such as greyhounds. The Afghan's coat is high maintenance, whereas the whippet's thin skin is vulnerable to scratches and gashes on the trail. Most hounds are a challenge to obedience train, and the whiff of an interesting scent can send them off wandering for hours. Short-legged breeds are not as well suited for long hikes over rugged terrain.

Spitz-Type Dogs
The plush coats of the smallest to the largest of this wolf-looking breed type indicate northern origins. The smaller breeds were bred to be companions, but the larger breeds hunted, herded, and pulled.

Breed examples: Alaskan malamute, Siberian husky, chow chow, Pomeranian.

Positive hiking traits: Well-balanced physical proportions also found in natural or primitive dogs; alert, active. The larger breeds have good endurance and are happiest when working. Carrying dog packs is a good substitute for pulling a sled or a cart.

Concerns: Thick coats make many breeds vulnerable to over-heating and restrict hiking to cooler high-country or winter conditions.

Terriers
Bred to track, tunnel out, and kill ground-burrowing mammals (rats, badgers, rabbits, foxes). They evolved from the hounds.

Breed examples: Scottish terrier, American pit bull terrier, dachshund.

Positive hiking traits: Robust, energetic. Some terriers have wiry coats that give them extra protection around dry, prickly brush.

Concerns: Some terriers are yappy, nippy, and can be belliger-ent around other dogs. Firm handling and obedience training are a must.

Sporting Group
This group was bred to find and retrieve game. Cooperation and responsiveness are two of the most valued traits in these breeds, which also make them popular family dogs.

Breed examples: retrievers, Brittany.

Positive hiking traits: Vigorous, generally gregarious, and easy to train. Dogs from this group display the best blend of desirable temperament and physical characteristics for the trail.

Concerns: If you are drawn to one of the very popular breeds, such as the Labradors and goldens, be very selective of the breeder. Sudden or extreme popularity of a breed often encour-ages indiscriminate breeding, which can result in an increase of physical and behavioral problems in some bloodlines.

Livestock

The livestock group is also known as the herding group. This working group was bred primarily to protect and/or herd the sheep, goats, and cattle with which they were raised. Some breeds are being successfully trained to transfer their guarding instincts to provide personal protection.

Breed examples: German shepherd, Australian shepherd, Old English sheepdog, Bernese.

Positive hiking traits: Herders of small to medium size are enthusiastic, athletic, outdoors-loving dogs that thrive on activity.

Concerns: The giant breeds, many used for draft or guard work in the mountains, have endurance, but many are afflicted with joint and bone problems that make them poor candidates for uphill hiking. Dogs bred for protection tend to have enhanced dominance. A hiker with such a dog should not be on the trail until the two have enough obedience training under their collars. The owner should be confident of his dog's reliability and of having the dog under control.

Companion Dogs

These dogs were originally, and some more recently, bred to be family companions.

Breed examples: bichon frise, pug, poodles, cockapoo.

Positive hiking traits: This group is the most diverse in physical appearance and disposition, which makes generalizations difficult. As long as you are realistic about the dog's physical abilities and limitations, a well-mannered dog that is a good companion at home can be trained to become a good companion on the trail. Toy-size fit breeds have the advantage of being portable when necessary. I recently met a spunky three-pound, seventeen-year-old Yorkshire terrier on the trail.

Concerns: A pampered indoor dog with high-maintenance grooming requirements may be less suitable for the great outdoors. You must be more vigilant with a small, bite-size dog to protect it from flying predators as well as those that stalk their prey. On one of our dog Shiloh's first hiking outings along an open ridge trail, we got quite a jolt. A large hawk swooped up the flank of the mountain, grazing Shiloh's thick-coated back close enough to roll her supple puppy body into a somersault a few feet ahead of us.

A Word about Hybrids and Controversial Breeds

There have been laws for many years in many states and municipalities prohibiting the ownership of hybrids (a cross between wolf or coyote and a domesticated breed such as a German shepherd or a husky). But now there is an increasing pressure to restrict or outlaw the ownership of pit bulls and other breeds of non-hybrid dogs considered "dangerous." Whether you're talking about hybrids or problematic breeds, there's always someone breeding them because there's always someone buying them.

People are often seduced by a hybrid's wild beauty. But the look isn't always all that's wild. While some domesticated dogs are a challenge, hybrids are often unmanageable.

Are hybrids reliable?

Reliable, no; predictable, yes. You can predict that at some point in a hybrid's life, under the right set of circumstances, his instincts will override socialization, domestication, and training. Speaking strictly of "trail" circumstances, a situation will come up where the hybrid will be torn between instinct and loyalty to his human. His unadulterated senses will drive him to chase prey as big as a deer until he takes it down or gives up on the brink of exhaustion. You can be left standing for minutes to days, voice commands trailing the wind.

A hybrid bred from a dog with strong guarding instincts (for instance, from a German shepherd) compounds the problem. Even if you use a leash conscientiously, passing hikers with other dogs on the narrow trails will be a challenge of control with a highly territorial hybrid dog.

Hybrids are trapped between domestic and wild, doomed to die from a bullet or to exist misunderstood and abused. With few exceptions, a hybrid's destiny is death or at best a life sentenced behind the chain-link fence of a rescue shelter. Humans are responsible for the problem, but ultimately the dogs bear the consequences.

Pit bull bashing

In the case of pit bulls, the problem is manmade. Too many have been bred and conditioned, often in cruel and inhumane environments, to reinforce aggressive traits, which, combined with their powerful jaws, makes them more of a concern than a snapping cocker spaniel. Aggressive, unpredictable dogs of *any* breed have no place on the trail.

Whether you feel that the pit bull hysteria is justified or just media hype, even the cutest pit bull puppy with no aggression tendencies or history will eventually grow into an adult that will be met with distrust by fellow hikers. What might be considered a posturing growl or a defensive nip from any other dog is likely to be interpreted as an act of aggression if it involves a pit bull or anything that looks like a pit bull.

With so many other options, you have to ask yourself is choosing a socially controversial breed for the public trails is worth the stress, risk, and potential consequences to you, your dog, and others on the trail. For more information, visit www.pitbull.us.

Physical traits that can be drawbacks

- Black coats absorb more heat and lead to overheating sooner than other dogs would experience.

- Thick coats can cause a dog to overheat more easily; they also become heavy when wet and can turn a tired dog into a drowning dog.

- Long coats or curly coats, like a Portuguese water dog's, can attract far more foxtails and burrs than shorter ones. (Consider a "trail trim" if you have a curly-coated or long-coated breed.)

- Hairless breeds are more susceptible to sunburn and cold. Sunscreen and doggie sweaters are essential accessories for these breeds.

- Short-legged dogs may have difficulty negotiating some trail conditions. This can slow your pace and affect the length of your hikes, so plan accordingly.

- Short-muzzled dogs (for example, pugs and boxers) are more susceptible to overheating during exertion because short sinus passages don't cool air as efficiently as longer ones.

Other Considerations

When selecting a dog for hiking, consider the animal's size, build, stamina, and temperament. But think too about your own personality and your lifestyle off the trail. To reduce the chances of making an impulsive and less-than-perfect choice, decide what you need in a dog, then start looking. Ask yourself the following questions to determine your needs:

- Do you have children?
- Do you have adequate indoor space for a dog?

- Do you have a fenced yard? Tying a dog to a chain is cruel and promotes aggressive behavior.
- Do you have time to train and care for a pet and to meet the dog's needs for exercise and mental stimulation off the trail?
- Do you have access to a park or natural area where your dog can romp, maintain his hiking form, and beat the boredom between hikes?
- Do you have the time or the budget for a dog with high-maintenance grooming requirements?
- Do you have the patience and schedule flexibility to commit to the needs of a puppy, or is an already housebroken and trained adult dog more suitable to your lifestyle? Breed rescue networks and shelters may have just the right adult dog for you.
- Do you have allergies? Pick a breed that does not shed.

Get Professional Input

Veterinarians, handlers, breeders, trainers, and groomers can give you valuable information during your quest for the ideal hiking dog. You can also check the library and bookstore for books and magazines about dogs.

Where to Look

Once you have narrowed down the breed or breed variety for the best match, where do you find that future hiking companion?

Breeders

If you want a purebred, start interviewing breeders. Word of mouth is the best source for a reputable breeder. You also can get the names of breeders from the vet, pet store, kennel clubs, and dog magazines. The right breeder will be concerned with a good match between dog and owner rather than a fast buck. He will interview you carefully and forthrightly. That breeder will keep puppies for about eight weeks, providing them with human companionship and regular exposure to household activity. Beware of breeders who seem eager to unload the puppies any sooner. The whelping or doggie nursery area should be clean and comfortable and reflect that the breeder cares about the animals. Ask to meet the pup's mother, as her appearance and disposition will tell you a lot about the puppies. If the male is not available, ask to talk to his owner and veterinarian.

Breed Rescue Clubs

Many breed clubs have a rescue network for their own breed. The network is a support system for dog owners who are no longer able to keep the dog, generally because of a change in personal circumstances. This can be a good source for someone who wants to bypass the trials and tribulations of puppy chewing and housebreaking by adopting a more mature dog that may even have had extensive training.

Animal Shelters

Visit your community animal shelter. Many wonderful purebreds and an even greater number of mixed breeds of different ages that deserve a good home are abandoned, lost, or given up to shelters daily. Some mixed breeds benefit from natural selection and display the best traits of their breed potpourri. If you find a dog that sparks your interest, get as much information as you can about the dog's breed or mix, background, and the reason the dog was given up for adoption. Talk to the shelter caretakers about their observations. Take the dog outside away from the chaos and stress of the shelter environment to interact with him and evaluate his disposition and your chemistry with him.

Pet Stores

These pet outlets shouldn't be your first choice. Pet stores can be a pipeline for backyard breeders and puppy mills, where dogs are bred indiscriminately and kept in pitiful conditions. Unless you can get a clear medical history on the puppy and specific breeder information to confirm its background, move on.

Newspapers

If you choose to look for a dog through the classifieds, keep the pet store guidelines in mind.

The More, the Merrier?

Two puppies are twice as cute and entertaining but double the trouble. Yes, they will keep each other company; however, they will be partners in crime, bonding to each other rather than to you, which will make them much less responsive to training. On the other hand, bringing a second dog into the household when the first is an adult (at least two years old) and well trained can be a lot of fun at home and on the trail. Dogs are pack animals. Even the presence of a pet of a different species can alleviate the solo dog's loneliness and boredom (the right cat often makes for a compatible companion).

A dog left alone for more than four hours needs access to a safe, fenced outdoor area. Anyone whose lifestyle requires a dog to be on its own for more than eight hours needs to reconsider taking on the responsibility of a dog.

Selecting a Specific Dog

The two most important qualities in any dog are a sound body and a sound mind. When you talk about choosing a dog that is compatible with all the variables of the "trail environment," you want to be able to screen the candidates as early as possible. Bloodline heredity and a thorough veterinary examination will give you a lot of tangible information about a dog's present and future physical condition.

Sitting in the middle of the room observing littermates and interacting with a pup can help you sort the shy from the bold, the dominant from the subordinate, and the independent from the responsive. But knowledge about a pup's critical developmental stages can help you evaluate whether a breeder is providing the proper environment and to assess a dog's risk of future behavioral problems.

Experts believe that a puppy's experiences during his first twelve weeks of life influence his potential to develop into a well-adjusted adult dog. A knowledgeable breeder can give your pup a head start toward healthy social skills.

Even if you have only limited or no information about how the dog was reared before it came to you, researching the developmental stages can help you cope with and correct some behavioral problems when and if they surface. (See *The Encyclopedia of the Dog,* listed in Appendix C.)

CHAPTER THREE

Bonding

Bonding is the loyalty, trust, and cooperation between you and your dog. A solid bond is crucial to successful training and fosters reliability on the trail. Bonding makes dogs more prone to please and therefore more likely to respond to commands. Nurturing the bond between you and your dog from the very beginning of your relationship will keep your dog behaving well on the trail.

Early Bonding

Socialization Period

Although there can be variations by breed and individuals, it is generally accepted that most puppies need to be with their mother until about eight weeks of age. The learning that occurs between mother and pup is one of the building blocks for a well-adjusted dog.

Puppies that engage in regular interactive play are smarter and settle easily in their slot of the pecking order because they have had plenty of opportunities to practice their social and communication skills. Dogs that are removed from the litter too young or are isolated from other dogs during this phase can later display excessive timidity or unprovoked aggression around other dogs.

Six to eight weeks is the peak age for human attachments. Pups need to be frequently handled by humans at this time. Introducing pups to new experiences during this phase—including the hum of daily household activity and basic training—will make future training easier.

Mature Bonding

After six to eight weeks of age, bonding occurs through consistent pleasurable interaction, including physical touch (petting to massaging), feeding, walking, playing, training, and positive reinforcement of desired behavior through rewards (verbal praise, stroking, and treats). The more timid the dog the more time, patience, and constant reassurance will be required to nurture it to some state of trust.

A dog regularly isolated in the yard, kennel, or a separate room can feel ostracized. Dogs need to be integrated in the daily activities of their human "pack" as much as possible. Hiking and backpacking excursions provide wonderful opportunities for quality bonding time.

Play

Play is natural and essential to dogs. A dog's first bonding experience and lessons in social behavior come through play with her littermates. Pups thrive on play physically and mentally. In addition to being a good bonding tool, play promotes social skills, agility, and resourcefulness. A hike can be a shared playtime between you and your dog. Experts warn against engaging in play-fighting with your dog during the socialization period, when you could be reinforcing dominance traits that could develop into aggression problems later.

Affection reinforces the bond between dog and owner.

Food

Food is another way to a dog's heart. Dogs bond more readily to a hand that feeds them. In the case of a shy dog, begin by hand-feeding a few bites before putting the food bowl down. Dogs are always enthusiastic about the humans who give them treats and throw tennis balls.

CHAPTER FOUR

Obedience

One of the gratifying aspects of obedience classes and hiking is that they complement each other. The drills prepare your dog, and the trail becomes a most enjoyable arena to practice and reinforce the classroom lessons. Obedience is especially important for a hiking dog because the nuisance and hazard of a few uncontrolled dogs can result in all dogs being banned from the trail.

Does Your Dog Need Obedience Training?

If the fact that basic obedience facilitates and enhances your relationship with your dog isn't motivation enough, realize that once you step out of your yard and onto the trail, everything your dog is and isn't reflects on you and impacts other people, animals, and the surrounding environment. Basic obedience skills are essential on the trail.

Vital aspects of your dog's trail education include:

1. Learning appropriate behavior around the people and animals on the trail.

2. Learning to respond to commands in spite of the naturally seductive sights, sounds, and smells of the trail.

3. Learning a repertoire of commands, including, at a minimum, *come*, *sit*, *down*, *stay* or *wait*, *heel*, *no*, and *leave it*.

Basic Commands

Use the word *off* when training your dog not to jump on people and dance on furniture. *Down* should be used strictly for laying down. It is unrealistic to expect an exuberant pup to respond to the *down* command under highly excitable circumstances. The best you can expect is for your dog to learn to display her excitement with all four paws touching the ground and stay *"off."* That drill, repeated over time, will prove to be one of your most challenging and rewarding accomplishments. Consistency and follow through in your drills, reinforced by praise and food reward, are essential.

Teach your dog that when you say "stay" or "wait" in the car, he should remain in the open vehicle until his leash is on and you've given the command that it's okay to jump out. The same thing applies to wanting your dog to learn impulse control—she should wait for your okay before sprinting and dashing off after you unleash her. The day will come when that simple command may save your dog's life.

Training Options

You can train your dog yourself. There are several good training books. You can find them at the library and at bookstores and pet supply stores. (See Appendix C for recommended reading.) The two main advantages of training your dog yourself are control of the training schedule and the minimal cost. The "do-it-yourself" method works best if you know and understand how a dog thinks and have the self-discipline to set aside about fifteen minutes twice a day to work with your dog.

Successful training is not measured just by the achieve-

A well-trained dog will avoid the instinctive impulse to chase wildlife.

ment of a dog's sitting, staying, and coming. The objective is to have your dog respond to commands with respectful but enthusiastic immediacy, rather than cowering compliance. Be careful with your dog's psyche. A novice dog owner with a well-intentioned trial-and-error approach can damage a dog's psyche just as easily as an experienced trainer who doesn't realize his methods are breaking the dog's spirit.

Calling your dog over to give him a reprimand is as counterproductive to fostering reliable off-leash recalls as sticking your pup's nose in his business is to housebreaking.

You might opt to enroll your dog in a group obedience class or to hire a private trainer. In teaching your dog commands for the trail, tone and verbal and body language can give a dog mixed or vague messages that confuse the dog, frustrate the owner, and undermine hiker/dog team spirit. A good trainer quickly gets the desired response from the dog (sitting, lying down, heeling). The trainer can teach the owner to communicate clearly, confidently, and in some cases assertively what he or she wants from the dog, all the while using humane, reward-based techniques.

A qualified trainer can help you work with and around your dog's natural instincts and breed characteristics so that traits like dominance, guarding and chasing instincts, independence, hyperalertness, or roaming do not become problems. A trainer can also instruct you in the appropriate use of tools such as the head halter, which is widely preferred over the less humane choke collar.

Group classes are often offered for a reasonable fee through local kennel clubs, pet supply stores, and veterinary clinics. Consider a puppy class or adult obedience class one of the best investments in your dog's and your relationship on the trail. Regardless of whether you are an experienced or first-time dog owner, the controlled but buzzing environment of a group class makes an excellent training ground for dogs to work on their social interaction with other dogs and humans, while learning to ignore distractions. Puppy classes have the advantage of training both pup and owner right out of the starting gate.

Private sessions can be more effective with dogs (especially adult dogs) and owners whose training needs require more one-on-one attention.

How Soon Should You Start Training Your Dog?

Although dogs are not admitted to puppy classes until they have had at least their first two DHLP-P (distemper/parvo) vaccinations (at about ten weeks), you should start working with your puppy on your own before that.

Basic training should start from the time the pup is born. Puppies that are handled by human hands earlier on bond more easily and accept human touch more readily. Practice calling your puppy enthusiastically to come and rewarding him with praise, petting, and a treat. This is the first step in many months of work toward every dog owner's ultimate goal—a reliable recall off leash. Never use your dog's name to reprimand, punish, or administer anything she views as unpleasant. The more pleasant the experience, the more reason to come quickly when you call her name.

CHAPTER FIVE

Training Tips and Tools

In the natural world, canines get their sense of security from pack order. The social order is essential to survival. It determines who breeds, leads, cares for the young, guards, and who eats when. It's instinctive in your dog, and he will be more responsive, calmer, happier, and better integrated in the family if his position in the pack is reaffirmed. Every pack needs an alpha, a leader but not a bully. You should be that leader.

The Importance of Being Consistent

Inconsistency breeds unpredictability. Rules and routine should be the same on the trail as they are at home. *No* should mean *no* anywhere. You don't want your dog testing you on the trail, where a rebellious act could put her life at risk or jeopardize someone else's safety.

Potty-Training Tip for the Trail

Conditioning your dog to relieve himself on command on leash is a housebreaking method that proves a valuable habit at roadside rest stops on the way to the trailhead or anytime you may need to monitor where your dog relieves himself during the hike. Begin at home by taking your dog outside on a leash at routine elimination times. Use a short command phrase like "go potty," "hurry up," "get busy," or any comfortable expression (English or foreign language). Use the expression as your dog relieves himself, avoiding an overzealous tone that could distract him from business. Reward your dog with a pat, enthusiastic praise, and a treat.

Crate Training

If used appropriately, a crate can be one of the most valuable training tools you'll ever own. Molded plastic airline-approved crates with side ventilation and a metal grate door with a latch have the most flexibility. They can be purchased at most airports from the airline, at pet supply stores, or from pet supply catalogs. This type is useful for housebreaking, easy to clean, and safe for transporting your dog in a vehicle and on airplanes. Lightweight canvas and mesh crates are also available and practical for home, car, or campground. In all probability, your dog will eventually experience the crate at the veterinarian's or the groomer's, so it's a good idea to familiarize him with it as soon as possible. The principles of crate training are the same regardless of your dog's age.

Proper training makes the crate a comfortable retreat.

What Size?

The crate should be large enough for the dog to lie, sit, stand, and move around comfortably with enough space for bedding (soft blanket or towel), a couple of toys, and a food and water dish. If you own a large breed, expect to upgrade the size of the crate at least a couple of times during the pup's growing months.

Four Steps to Successful Crate Training

The goal is to help your dog think of the crate as his den, a safe, clean, comfortable place where he feels relaxed and content, not incarcerated.

1. The crate should always be kept (day and night) where your dog can feel like part of the family. Remember that dogs are social animals and that isolation from the family in the laundry room, the garage, or the yard makes them feel like they are being ostracized from the "pack" and punished. Between six and eight weeks, pups should sleep next to their owner's bed (in the crate).

2. Initially place the crate, with door open, wherever the dog is most likely to investigate it.

3. After a good play session and a romp outside to relieve himself, encourage your dog to explore the inside of the crate, where he'll find his blanket, toys, treats, and whatever particulars make the crate a pleasant place.

4. Place your dog's food dish at the back of the crate and feed one or two meals a day in the crate with the door open for about a week or until your dog is comfortable entering and leaving the crate. Later, close the door for a short while, gradually increasing your dog's time in the crate.

5. Pups less than four months should not be left alone or in the crate more than two hours at a time. On the road, dogs of any age should be taken out of the crate at least every couple of hours.

Pack Training:

Day hikes should be carefree, travel-light fun. Overnight trips require significantly more gear, which is an opportunity to give fit adult medium-to-large dogs (more than thirty-five pounds) the sense of purpose so many thrive on. With patient and proper training these enthusiastic bundles of dog muscle power can learn to carry food and backpacking accessories.

It is important to emphasize that loaded packs should only be carried by adult dogs that have reached full physical matu-

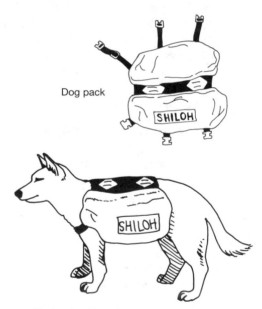

Dog pack

Packs should conform to your dog's build.

rity. The total weight on your dog's back should not exceed a quarter to a third of its weight (a forty-pound dog should not carry more than ten to thirteen pounds of evenly distributed weight). Begin by placing a face cloth or small towel on your dog's back to introduce your dog to the feel of weight on his back. Leave the pack around the house near his bed or crate for a few days and in the car when you take him for a ride.

Feed him little treats while you try the pack on him (empty), and praise him for having the pack on. Take it off and repeat the exercise twice a day for about a week.

The next step is to put the pack on for going on a leash walk. Give him the treat while you are putting the pack on, and then put his leash on as you would on a regular walk.

Put the pack on for short hikes with only treats in the pouches, so you can take the treats from his pack on snack breaks. The idea is to create positive associations with the pack so that eventually the sight of the pack evokes an enthusiastic response from your dog.

Antibark Collars

A barking dog is an intrusion in nature. If barking is going to be a problem, consider a citronella spray antibark collar—it is more humane than the traditional shock collar. Barking triggers the release of a burst of lemon-scented spray under your dog's nose. The unpleasant and startling citrus spray eliminates barking with most dogs. (Collars and refills are available from some veterinarians, trainers, pet stores, and mail order catalogs.)

Getting to the Trail Safely

Maybe traveling hasn't been part of your dog's lifestyle until now, but chances are your hiking excursions will involve some vehicle travel time. Ideally, your vehicle should be large enough to accommodate a dog crate or a dog barrier so that both dog and passengers are safe and comfortable. Dogs hopping between the front and back seats are a distraction and hazard to the driver; dogs bouncing in the bed of pickup trucks are at risk of serious injury.

- Never put the crate or the dog in direct sunlight.
- Provide adequate ventilation and remember that in the summertime, cracking the window is *never* enough, even on a cloudy day.
- Offer your dog water at every stop.
- Train yourself to leash your dog before you open the car door.
- Train your dog to *wait* or *stay* in the crate or in the vehicle until you leash and invite him out with a command like *okay* or *hop out*. These can be life-saving communication cues.

All Aboard

Initially, the vehicle should be stationary in the garage or driveway. Turn on the engine and sit for a few times. Next is the short drive down the street with the stop for a walk or a play session to promote the positive association with the car ride. Getting in the car only for veterinarian visits is a sure way to sabotage your road training efforts.

Once you feel confident that your dog is comfortable riding in the car, take her with you around town as often as you can: stop at the park for a walk or even stroll through your local pet supply store for a biscuit. Drive smoothly, avoid winding roads, and gradually increase the length of the drives between routine stops.

Remember to make frequent stops on longer road trips for stretching and sniffing and offer your dog water at every stop.

Motion Sickness

Dogs prone to motion sickness should not be fed on the morning of the drive; instead feed them an hour after arrival or when they seem recovered from the stress of the drive. Food and hyperventilation can be an uncomfortable-to-dangerous combination, especially for large breeds with a predisposition to bloating. (See Chapter 7.)

Consult your veterinarian about the appropriate use of Dramamine to treat motion sickness and certain antihistamines for their calming effects, as opposed to medications that sedate.

Cool Ride

Make your dog more comfortable during a hot drive to and from the trailhead by covering his bedding with a wet towel, or placing soft ice packs under a towel. Water-absorbent crate mats are available through mail-order catalogs. Never leave your pet unattended in a vehicle for more than a very few minutes, and take a moment to slip a foldable sun-reflecting shield inside your windshield any time you park the car with your dog in it. It takes only a few minutes for your car to become a deadly oven, even with windows cracked.

CHAPTER SIX

Conditioning Your Dog

Preparing your dog for hiking is like coaching an athlete for an Olympic decathlon. You must get her in good physical condition (muscular and cardiovascular) to enjoy the hike safely. Certain parts of your dog's body will require special care and attention before hiking to prevent injury or discomfort. Mental conditioning includes familiarizing him with hiking equipment and the trail environment.

Conditioning will enhance your dog's fitness for the trail.

Prehike Care

Dewclaws: All dogs are born with front dewclaws, and many have rear dewclaws. This fifth digit on the inside of the leg is very prone to tearing and ideally should be removed by a veterinarian within a few days after birth. If dewclaws have not been removed, consider having this surgery done at the same time your dog is spayed or neutered.

Nails: Nails should be comfortably short without sacrificing traction. Even dogs that are active enough outdoors to keep their nails naturally worn need to have the nail on the dewclaw trimmed. Consult a groomer or your veterinarian on the proper use of dog nail clippers and nail file for maintenance between clips.

Feet: Dog footpads get toughened (light sandpaper texture) by regular and gradual extended walks and runs on rough and varied surfaces (pavement, sand, and rocks). Booties should be worn to alleviate tenderness and protect footpads from cuts on ice and sharp rocks

Spaying and neutering: Your dog will be just as smart, loving, and trim after he or she is altered. Altering does not make dogs fat. Too much food and too little exercise do. Besides some of the social and medical benefits of altering, which include a reduced incidence of mammary gland cancer in females and prostate cancer in males, a decreased sexual drive will make your pet less apt to roam or tangle with other dogs. The trail advantage of neutering is a male dog that is more congenial and less preoccupied with competition around other males.

Vaccinations: Your dog should be current on all vaccinations (DHLP-P, rabies, and a vaccination against Lyme disease are advisable). The veterinary community's thinking on annual vaccines has evolved over the last few years, and many veterinarians now customize vaccine regimens to the individual dog, taking into account age and lifestyle. Discuss these changes with your veterinarian. Also ask him or her about the recent vaccine against rattlesnake venom.

Heartworm: Mosquitoes carry this parasite. Consult your veterinarian about heartworm preventive medication.

West Nile virus: Mosquitoes carry this virus. At this time there have been no reports of noticeable symptoms or fatal infections in canines. No vaccine or specific treatment exists.

Fleas and ticks: Dogs can be infected with tapeworms by ingesting fleas that are carriers of tapeworm eggs. Some types of ticks are carriers of disease (see Chapter 9). There is a bigger arsenal of flea and tick products on the market than ever. Consult your veterinarian on the treatment of choice for your dog and his hiking needs.

Grooming: Long coats should be trimmed (not shaved), particularly under the belly and behind the legs during the summer. Trimming hair between the toes prevents foxtails (invasive grasses found primarily in the western U.S.) from going undetected while they burrow, puncture, and infect. In the winter, less hair between the toes prevents the formation of icicles around the pads, decreasing the chance for frostbite.

Building Confidence

Exposure to the trail environment at an early age (preferably before twelve weeks) will help build your dog's confidence. Dogs get comfortable with sounds, sights, and experiences by early and constant exposure as pups (ideally before sixteen weeks old). Beyond four months of age, new experiences are met with a degree of natural apprehension and caution. If your dog has already developed a fear of certain situations, you will need to recondition her by introducing the threatening stimuli gradually and in small doses. This is often typical of the more primitive breeds and particularly hybrids, whose acute survival instincts prevent them from taking the new and unusual in stride.

On the other hand, this kind of environmental hyperawareness can become an asset on the trail. Such a dog may sense and communicate real dangers to you before you even see, hear, or feel the hint of a threat. He may be the one to smell or see the bear, hear the landslide, or feel a precarious situation developing.

Trail Sights

Let your dog get used to seeing backpacks, walking sticks, tents, and other hiking equipment around the house. Simulate trail circumstances by having friends with backpacks, walking sticks, and fishing rods stroll around the yard or come around the corner while you are on a walk with your dog. By the time you head for the trail, strangers waddling toward your dog in full backcountry outfits will not cause retreat or barking. There may be horses, pack stock, and cyclists on the trail, so introduce your dog to these ahead of time.

Building Stamina

Puppies Eight to Sixteen Weeks Old

Even a big backyard can be full of adventures and exploration possibilities for a pup. It's a good idea to introduce your pup to the natural hiking setting as early as possible, but you must be sensible about her vulnerability to infectious diseases. Pups get their initial immunity from their mother's milk, but they need protection through inoculation after they stop nursing.

By twelve weeks, your pup should have had the first of three DHLP-P vaccinations. Although it may be reasonably safe to socialize and romp around other pups on the same vaccination schedule, hold off on the great outdoors until she has had her final series of DHLP-P and rabies vaccination (four to six months). Try to take her to a park, beach, or neighborhood trail for exercise and sensory stimulation (twenty- to thirty-minute sessions) in addition to playtime and at least two leash walks daily. Use good sense and don't expose your pup to strange dogs or other animals until she has been vaccinated against rabies.

Puppies Four to Six Months Old

By now your puppy should be fully immunized and can safely venture away from the grassy green belts of civilization and closer to nature. Fields, meadows, or nearby forested trails will be more stimulating for your pup, although the distractions will make training more challenging for both of you.

Use a long rope or expandable leash (20 to 30 feet) so your pup can romp and explore under controlled conditions. Practice *sit*, *stay*, *down*, and *come* at the end of the rope several times. Let him off in a safe area of the trail and practice calling him enthusiastically during these prehike drills, rewarding him with a "good dog" a pat, and treats. Always use verbal praise and a pat, and when the desired behavior becomes consistent, use food rewards only some of the time.

Tell your dog to go play and do not call him unless you have eye contact or know you have his attention. When he is busy smelling, listening, or digging for creatures, he does not hear you. Do not compete and set yourselves up for failure. Never call him to you for a reprimand, no matter how frustrated you may be with his behavior.

These introductory training excursions (30 minutes to one

hour) will leave an overactive puppy calm and sleepy for his indoor life. Remember that during the first several months (six for small dogs, nine to twelve for larger dogs), most of the dog's energy is going into the growth of his young body. Do not stress the healthy development of your dog's muscles and bones with long distances and hills. With giant breeds, until twelve to eighteen months, keep the excursions short (under an hour) and on mostly flat terrain.

Take frequent rest stops and water breaks. In warm weather, stop every twenty minutes for your puppy to rest and drink water.

Adult Dogs

Gradual conditioning principles also apply to adult dogs that are just being introduced to the fun of hiking. If your dog's arena of physical activity has been primarily in the yard, begin by planning a walking route that allows you to be out thirty minutes twice daily (morning and evening). Following is an example of a five-week training program that can be adapted to your lifestyle and your dog's fitness level. Consult your physician and your veterinarian before making any changes to your and your dog's physical activity level.

Week 1 Morning and Evening	15-minute sniff and stroll (warm-up) 10-minute brisk walk (cardiovascular workout) 5-minute sniff and stroll (cool down)
Week 2 Morning and Evening	15-minute sniff and stroll (warm-up) 20-minute brisk walk (cardiovascular workout) 5-minute sniff and stroll (cool down)

continued

Week 3 Morning and Evening	15-minute sniff and stroll (warm-up) 20-minute brisk walk (cardiovascular workout) 5-minute sniff and stroll (cool down)
Week 4 Morning and Evening	15-minute sniff and stroll (warm-up) 30-minute brisk walk (cardiovascular workout) 10-minute stroll and sniff (cool down)
Week 5 Morning and Evening	15-minute sniff and stroll (warm-up) 30-minute brisk walk (cardiovascular workout) 10-minute sniff and stroll (cool down) One additional longer walk at end of week (about 1.5 hours)

The suggested longer walk at the end of week 5 is about increasing distance, not speed. Consider using this Week 5 regimen as a guideline for maintaining your dog's conditioning between hikes.

Once you both feel reasonably fit, incorporate some stairs or a hill to train for the up-and-down of backcountry trails. Ideally, your dog should be getting at least two hours of outdoor exercise daily, including walks and off-leash playtime. Make sure she always has drinking water, shade, and rest as needed.

During the summer months, shade from trees or cooling off in surface water helps dogs regulate their body temperature. If your dog decides to lounge in a mud puddle, let her. A dirty dog is the least of your worries. (See Chapter 11.)

Pacing

A person of average physical fitness walks about 3 miles per hour on a paved level path. To get a better idea of your and your dog's average stride and pace, time yourself walking around the local high school running track with your dog on leash. (Tracks are 0.25 mile per lap.) Keep in mind that on a hike, the terrain, weather, elevation, and steep climbs will affect your pace. In the mountains, for every 1,000 feet of elevation gain you can add 1 extra mile to the original length of the hike. Contrary to what many people think, hiking downhill is not twice as fast as hiking uphill. It takes about three-quarters of the time to hike the same distance downhill.

Health Considerations

Seriously and realistically consider your dog's age and current physical condition. This is not to say that if your dog is older, overweight, or has a medical condition she cannot hike. But if common sense precludes a human couch potato from sprinting a mile or driving to 8,000 feet for a 5-mile hike, the same applies to a dog who divides his time between the yard and his dog bed.

Consult your veterinarian to help evaluate your dog's health and discuss under what conditions hiking would be beneficial.

CHAPTER SEVEN

Day Hike Gear

There are certain necessary items to make your day hikes safe and more enjoyable with your dog. The following list describes gear options that can further increase your safety and that of your dog and enhance your hiking experience. Many of the day hike equipment items are essential building blocks to a successful backpacking excursion (see Chapter 8).

Collars and Harnesses

Either a collar or harness is suitable, but a colorful harness makes your dog more visible and identifies him as domestic. For dogs of intimidating size or appearance, a colorful harness emphasizes their pet status. It is easier to restrain a dog by a harness than a collar when necessary. In addition, a harness is a safer restraint (a collar could slip off or choke the animal) if your dog were ever in a predicament requiring you to pull him out of water or hoist him up a hillside. Harnesses are safer than collars off-leash because they reduce the risk of neck injury or suffocation from a snag or tangle in brush or a branch. With an adult dog who insists on pulling you along, the harness will give you more control and prevent damage to his neck and throat.

Fabric: Although leather is the most durable, nylon collars and harnesses are available in vibrant colors, are usually adjustable, and dry more quickly and without shrinkage. Your dog is less likely to lose a collar or harness with a plastic snap-in clasp than a metal buckle when he's running, swimming, and jostling about.

Fit: You should be able to easily slip your flat hand under the collar and rotate the collar; however, the collar should not be so loose that it can slip over the dog's head. A puppy will need to be fitted with a new collar a few times as he grows. Harnesses need to fit loosely enough to allow full expansion of the chest and a free stride.

Many trainers now consider choke collars an inhumane training tool, and a choke collar as a permanent collar can be *deadly*. To mention a few scenarios, strangulation has occurred when another dog's jaw has gotten twisted in the choke collar during rambunctious play; a dog has snagged his choke collar on a low branch while running through the brush; and a dog has slipped and fallen off a porch or a boulder, hanging himself at the end of a leash and choke collar.

Harness

Identification Tags

On the trail a tag is the most obvious way to reunite a lost dog and its owner. The information should at least include the dog's name (first and last name), home telephone number with area code, cell phone number, and street address (not a P.O. box). The sight, smell, or sound of another animal could lure your dog away, and thunder or gunshots could startle your dog and cause her to run off. Whatever the reason for the separation, you want to facilitate a reunion. If another person gets close enough to your dog to see the tag, the first thing he or she will look for is a name. Calling the dog by its name will establish some communication and trust. The telephone number allows the finder to leave a message with someone in your household or on your answering machine.

Temporary identification: In addition to her permanent tag, your dog needs a temporary identification tag when you are hiking out of town. The tag should have the dates and telephone number of when and where you are staying in the area, (campground, friend's house, or hotel) and your cell phone number. If you are on a day hike, write the name of the trail, your destination, and the trailhead where you are parked.

Securing the tag: Loop rings are more secure than S rings for attaching tags. Small plastic luggage tags on a loop ring make inexpensive reusable temporary tags.

Lobo Mullally
Home: 555–458–4617
Cell: 555–314–0002

An identification tag is a must.

Leashes

A leash that will suffer the abuse of the trail (streams, rain, snow, and rocks) must be durable. On the one hand, a color nylon webbed leash is light, dries quickly, and is easy to spot when you lay it down. You can design your own leash inexpensively by buying the webbed nylon by the foot at a mountaineering store and the clasp at a hardware store.

On the other hand, leather leashes stay the cleanest and last forever. Place a piece of colored tape or tie a strand of colored fabric to the handle to make finding the leash easier when it is on the ground. Leather leashes are often required in obedience classes.

If you are hiking in a strictly on-leash environment, expandable leashes blend control and freedom. The leashes come in varied lengths and strengths based on dog weight. An expandable leash can also convert into a tie-out line.

Bandannas

A colorful bandanna around a dog's neck sends two important messages. It can say "cute," which helps make big dogs look less intimidating to those hikers who may be fearful of them. In the forest, a bright bandanna also says "domestic," which

A bandanna around the neck can send an important signal on the trail.

helps distinguish dogs from game during the hunting season. For extra visibility, tie the bandanna on a colorful harness.

Reflective Vest

If you are going to hike during hunting season, your dog should wear a bright lightweight, reflective vest, designed for sporting dogs. This will help distinguish your dog from wildlife.

Booties

If your dog is only an occasional hiker who spends most of his time sauntering across the lawn at home, his pads may get tender after even just a couple of miles. Booties can give relief to your dog's sore paws until his pads toughen, as well as prevent cuts from crusty or icy trail conditions. Your dog should practice wearing booties at home before using them on the trail.

Where to buy booties: Booties come in different sizes and materials and are available through pet supply stores, mail-order catalogs, and mountaineering stores and are advertised in dog sledding magazines.

Booties help protect tender paws.

Dog Packs

Although it is a good idea to introduce young dogs to the idea of packs, loaded packs should be used only on fit adult, medium-to-large dogs (thirty-five pounds or more). The pack weight *should not exceed* one-quarter to one-third of your dog's weight. (For example, a forty-pound dog should not carry more than ten to thirteen pounds of evenly distributed weight.)

Most packs are designed to lay on the dog's back like a saddle with a pouch on each side. Packs are more appropriate for overnight trips than day hikes, and should only be carried by fit medium-to-large adult dogs. (See Chapter 5 for pack training information.). There's significantly more gear when you go overnight, and it's a good use of dog power to train a medium- or large-size dog to assist by carrying her booties, first-aid kit, food, and treats or other accessories related to her needs.

Choosing packs: Packs are sold in pet supply stores, outdoor recreation stores, and mail-order catalogs. They come in different sizes with adjustable straps. Look for the design that best conforms to your dog's body. The pack should feature breathable material, rounded corners, and padding for additional comfort.

Pack fitting: Your dog's comfort depends on a proper fit. The pack sits on his shoulders between the base of the neck and short of the hips. There should be one strap that clips on the front of his chest and one or two belly straps to stabilize the pack. Straps should be tight enough to keep the pack in place but loose enough to allow full stride without chafing and comfortable expansion of the chest for breathing. (See Appendix B for suggested dog pack sources.)

Loading the packs: Stuff the packs with crumpled newspaper at first. Then, once he is accustomed to the packs and his endurance is built up, gradually increase the load from 10 percent of his weight not to exceed one-quarter to one-third of his weight. If you use packs only occasionally, keep the weight on the lighter side. The weight should be equal and evenly distributed to avoid interfering with your dog's balance.

Pack Safety

Keep your dog on leash when he is wearing his packs. Packs can make balance awkward when negotiating narrow mountainside trails or crossing fast streams. Give him a break every hour or so by removing the packs so he enjoys the freedom you both came for by playing, swimming, and rolling around without risking injury to himself and damage to his packs and cargo.

Life Vest

A life vest is important to have if you are going to hike near rivers and lakes or if you have to cross high water, especially with dogs who are drawn to water. An elderly or tired dog is more at risk in the water during a hike than she would be at the beach for the day.

Flashlight and Extra Batteries

You will be thankful for a flashlight—especially one that fits in a day pack—if you are still hiking after sunset.

Matches and Cigarette Lighter

Temperatures can drop quickly after the sun goes down. If you are lost or injured, a fire can help keep you warm until daylight or help arrives. Put matches and a strike strip in a pill bottle to protect them from the elements. Gas clicker lighters are lightweight and can be easier to use in inclement weather.

Lightweight Nylon Tarp

In an emergency, a tarp makes a lightweight shelter from sun, wind, and rain. Purchase a lightweight one at a local hardware or outdoor store.

Flyers for a Lost Dog

Carry a few photocopied flyers with your dog's photo, name, and a contact phone number. If the unfortunate happens, you can fill in a description of the area where your dog was lost and post flyers at the trailhead, campground, and ranger station and carry one to show to other hikers along the way.

Food

Dogs require a balanced diet made up of five essential nutrients: protein, fat, carbohydrates, minerals, and vitamins.

Types of Food

Human food (cooked poultry, meat, and rice) is tasty and freshest but requires more preparation and planning. Commercial dog food comes moist (canned), semimoist (sealed pouches), and dry.

Dry kibble is convenient but should be supplemented with a dab of healthy, nutritious, and tasty human food or quality canned dog food.

Read the ingredients and choose a premium brand from the supermarket or pet supply store, avoiding brands with animal by-products and corn fillers. Choose a formula that matches your dog's age group and activity level, such as puppy growth, adult maintenance, high performance, and senior for less active dogs.

Dogs with restricted diets due to medical conditions or allergies are often fed "prescription" brands obtained from a veterinarian. The breeder and your veterinarian can help guide you in choosing appropriate foods for your dog.

Feeding My Dog

Puppies are generally fed three or four smaller meals per day. Just as smaller, more frequent meals are healthier for humans, adult dogs should be fed at least twice a day. To do this, divide their total daily portion into two smaller meals (morning and evening). Exercising on a full stomach is uncomfortable because most of the body's blood supply is busy helping with digestion rather than supplying oxygen to the muscles and the cardiovascular system.

It is not necessary to increase your dog's amount of food for a day hike. Instead, supplement his diet at snack breaks. Pack dog biscuits, jerky treats, and a pouch of semimoist food or extra dry kibble. Some dogs like carrots, apples, and melon pieces as much as any canine treat. (Never feed chocolate to dogs. It is toxic.)

In cold weather, bring higher-protein dog snacks. Look for real liver, turkey, chicken, or egg as the first ingredient and avoid products with sugar and fillers. (See Chapter 8 for back-packing feeding tips.)

Food/Exercise Risks

There are differing theories on the condition called gastric dilatation-volvulus complex (GDV), which involves bloating and stomach torsion. The most popular explanation suggests that strenuous exercise (jumping and running) after a large meal may compound the risks of the stomach twisting in the abdomen, blocking the flow or absorption of gastric material. Large breeds are especially prone to GDV, which can be fatal. Dividing daily portions into smaller, more frequent meals, preferably fed during rest periods on the trail or in camp, can help prevent GDV.

Plastic Resealable Bags

The airtight, self-sealing invention is in the top five essentials for the trail. These bags are great for carrying food, treats, medication, and first aid necessities, and they can easily be converted into food and water bowls. Their "sealing" quality comes in handy for disposing of dog waste.

Water

Water is as essential to your dog as it is to you. Do not skimp on bringing water or count on finding it along the trail. Dehydration can result in sluggishness, kidney problems, and heat stroke. Both humans and dogs are vulnerable to dehydration in the heat and at high elevations.

Do not let your dog drink from standing water in puddles, ponds, lakes, or swimming holes in slow-moving creeks and rivers. That's where different forms of bacteria and algae breed, and small dogs and puppies have been known to get very ill and in some cases die from drinking contaminated water. Be especially wary of areas where cattle graze.

Both dogs and humans are susceptible to the intestinal parasite *Giardia lamblia*, which can cause cramping and diarrhea, leading to serious dehydration. *Giardia* can be present in all sources of untreated water.

How Much Water Do I Need?

Carry at least eight ounces of water per dog per hour of hiking. Consider that an average walking pace on level ground is about 3 miles per hour. Fill plastic water bottles (three-quarters full) and place in the freezer the night before. Your dog will have a source of cool fresh water as the ice melts along the way. Two frozen water bottles can also keep her cooler if you place one in each pouch of her dog pack.

Offer your dog water frequently (every half hour or more

on hot days). It is easier to regulate hydration with regular small intakes of water.

Snow may keep your dog cool, but do not believe that a hot, thirsty dog will instinctively know to eat snow to quench her thirst. One hiker reported that her southern California-born-and-raised dog was almost delirious from dehydration after she took him on a summer hike up a mountain where she thought the abundant snow would make up for the lack of water.

Bowls

Weight and encumbrances are the main concerns when packing for a hike. There are plenty of ways to create inexpensive doggie dinnerware on the trail. Paper or plastic picnic plates and bowls are lightweight and adequate for food and water. A plastic resealable bag can store the kibble and convert into a food dish or water bowl (hold the bag while your dog drinks from it). Pet supply stores and mail-order catalogs have several doggie gadgets for carrying and serving food and water on the trail, from canteens to collapsible bowls.

First-aid Kit

Although you cannot prepare for all the mishaps, it is best to have a few first-aid items. See Appendix A for a list of items to help you cope with some common injuries and nuisances on the trail. Also see Appendix A for a more detailed checklist of day hiking gear.

CHAPTER EIGHT

Backpacking Gear

Maybe it's the thought of retreating deeper into the solitary beauty of the wilderness with your four-legged companion that draws you. Or perhaps you're satisfied with setting up camp a few miles up the trailhead to share an easy, idyllic overnight in the great outdoors with him. Whichever appeals to you, back-packing with your dog requires some extra necessities and

The comforts of camp are many.

additional planning. Your goal is to travel light while considering emergencies, outdoor dining pleasures, and sleeping comforts for both you and your dog. Refer to Chapter 7 and Appendix A for a basic gear discussion and checklist, but add the following things to your list for a backpacking adventure.

Permits

Permits are generally obtained from ranger stations of the government agency that manages the land you wish to hike on (e.g., national or state park and forest, Bureau of Land Management). Permits are usually required for overnights in wilderness areas and in other heavily used recreation areas. In some places, registering or obtaining a permit can be required even for day hiking. In areas where use is strictly regulated, you may have to apply for a permit several months ahead of time.

Food

Make a list of the number of meals and snacks per hiking day for you and your dog. Package your dog's meals and snacks (preferably dry or semimoist) individually in resealable bags for convenience and to keep food smells from attracting bears.

You can safely supplement your dog's dry kibbles with most human food you would bring for yourself, except sugar and chocolate (chocolate is toxic to dogs as well as cats). Plan to take one extra cup of human food per day to supplement your dog's dinner in camp. Pasta and rice are lightweight and easy to cook in camp and can be prepared creatively for extra taste and nutrition.

Meat eaters can add canned tuna or chicken, as well as any freeze-dried meat sauce or soup mix. Either way, your dog will appreciate the added flavor to her kibbles and will benefit from the energy fuel. (Note: Introduce her to new foods at home gradually before going on the trail.)

Cutting your dog's regular dog food with puppy food will add the extra protein and fat needed for the higher calorie-burning excursions. Begin mixing in small amounts of puppy food about three days before the hike so your dog's digestive system can adapt gradually.

Water

You need to take enough water for drinking (for you and the dog) and cooking. If you are sure of the availability of water, consider carrying less and boiling, filtering, or chemically treating the water in camp. There are several water purification systems available at outdoor recreation stores, but be aware that some dogs will not drink chemically treated water.

Bedding

For yourself, choose a sleeping bag rated to keep you warm in the region and season in which you are backpacking.

For your dog, carry a piece of foam and a towel, which you can roll up with your sleeping bag. Or try a lightweight dog bedroll, designed to be cuddly on one side and durable on the side in contact with the ground; dog bedrolls are available in pet supply stores and through mail-order catalogs.

If you choose to sleep under the stars, make sure your dog is staked on a line (6-foot radius from his stake or tree) short enough to keep him away from the campfire but long enough to allow him to have physical contact with you. Physical con-

Collapsible
bowl

Bedroll

Tie-out line

tact gives your dog the security that will help keep him quieter if the sounds of the dark outdoors are new to him. It enables you to hush him at the first hint of a growl, keeps him warmer on cold nights, and lets you know when he's on alert.

Shelter

A tent gives you more protection from the elements and the wilderness nightlife. Buy one that can accommodate your dog. As a guideline, some of the lightweight three-person dome tents are roomy enough to fit two medium-size dogs as well. Dogs that are used to indoor creature comforts will want to and should sleep in the tent. Even inside the tent, your dog will alert you to suspicious sounds and smells.

If your dog is larger, thick-coated, and happier outside, still tie him close enough to keep him safe and reassured. Do not tie him to the tent—if your dog lunges at something, part of your tent will go with him.

Setting Up Camp

Evening

1. Pick your campsite in daylight, taking into account exposure, water, mosquitoes, and your dog's comfort.

2. Put your dog on her tie-out line, where she can curl up to rest, and give her water while you set up camp (sleeping and cooking quarters). Keep her water bowl full, within easy reach but out of the "step and spill" zone.

3. Get enough water to boil or filter for cooking dinner and break-fast, and enough drinking water for you and pooch for the evening and following trail day (eight ounces per mile per dog).

4. Prepare dinner for you and pooch.

5. Wash the dishes and burn or seal garbage in plastic bags for

pack-out to remove any food smells from camp. Be sure to use the bear-proof metal food storage bins whenever provided, and consider buying your own small bear-proof canisters for your aromatic goods.

6. Walk your dog before bedtime, tidy up camp, and snuggle up for the night.

Morning

7. Walk your dog and clean up any of her waste.

8. Share a hot breakfast with her (instant hot cereal or scrambled eggs over her kibble, with a hot drink for you and warm water for her).

9. Clean up and pack up. Leave your campsite cleaner than you found it.

Three reasons why your dog should be attended in camp at all times

1. He would be vulnerable to wild predators otherwise.

2. It would be unfair to cause him stress from being separated from you in unfamiliar surroundings.

3. Separation anxiety is often expressed through barking, whining, and howling, which ruins the wilderness experience for other campers. Do not forget that separation anxiety could bring on a chewing rampage that might leave you with a shredded tent, sleeping bag, or backpack.

With good planning and careful attention to gear, backpacking can heighten the pleasures of the trail for your and your dog. (For a detailed backpacking checklist, see Appendix A.)

CHAPTER NINE

On the Trail

Every hike shares routine preparations, but some destinations require more specific planning. In addition, the coast, mountains, desert, and forest offer different sources of enjoyment as well as challenges that can affect your dog.

General Considerations

Always get information ahead of time about the area where you want to hike.

Are dogs allowed? Determine which agency regulates the area (national, state, regional, or other), call ahead for its restrictions about dogs on the trails, and abide by the rules.

Do you need a permit? Call the managing agency about its regulations.

What kind of weather can you expect? The high country is subject to more variable and extreme weather. Check the weather forecast and fire danger advisory at a ranger station. Afternoon thunderstorms in the summer are common, and it is best to be below the timberline and off exposed ridges. In the spring and fall, pay attention to sudden drops in temperature and clouds moving in announcing snowfall.

What are the trail conditions? Advisories about fast water, high streams, and trail damage are commonly posted at a ranger station or visitor center. If nothing is posted, ask anyway.

What is the terrain like? A topographic map is an indispensable tool in planning your hike. Learn to read the information. A topographic map indicates boundaries between public lands and private lands and clearly shows marked trails and campgrounds. It shows you the elevation changes and how hilly or flat the surrounding terrain may be, so you can anticipate the difficulty of the trail and pace yourself appropriately. Every 1,000 feet of elevation equals about 1 extra mile of hiking. The map shows you if there is surface water (lakes, streams, and rivers) along the way. Studying the topographic map of the region beforehand allows you to choose the most appropriate trail for your dog's comfort and safety and to pack accordingly. Forests mean more shade; open ridge trails mean potential exposure to the elements (heat of the day, wind, and lightning); meadows mean mosquitoes; streams, rivers, and lakes indicate cooling stops. Topographic maps are for sale at some bookstores, ranger stations, park visitor centers, outdoor recreation stores and on the Internet. (See Appendix C.)

GPS (global positioning system) technology gives your current and precise location. It is rapidly evolving for affordable consumer use as a battery-operated handheld navigational tool. If you are "gadget-happy," there is a growing array of sophisticated GPS devices that interface with computer programs. They allow you to map out distance and elevation changes, view the route from a flyover perspective, and store and print the data. On a less intimidating level, the average hiker can easily learn to use a basic GPS in conjunction with a topographic map for more precise navigation.

What wildlife can you expect? You will want to know about bears, mountain lions, rattlesnakes, or other creatures that may be a safety concern to you and your dog.

What if something happens to you? Leave a copy of your itinerary with a friend or family member. Use their name and contact number on your dog's temporary ID and the lost dog flyer.

Seasonal Considerations

Summer heat can be taxing on your dog. The dry heat of the West, however, is more tolerable than the humidity of the South and East.

Minimizing Dehydration and Heat Stroke Risk

1. Hike in the early morning or late afternoon.
2. Carry at least eight ounces of water per dog for each hour on the trail or 3 miles of hiking.
3. Rest in a shaded area during the intensity of the midday.
4. Take frequent rest stops and offer your dog water.
5. Let him take a plunge in the lake or lie belly-down in a stream or mud puddle to cool.

Winter conditions will affect your dog's feet, her endurance, and her body warmth. Crusty snow can chafe and cut her pads, and walking in deep snow is very taxing and can put a short-haired dog at risk of hypothermia and frostbite.

Snow Safety

1. Carry booties for icy conditions and use them on dogs not accustomed to winter conditions. Take a couple of extras as replacements for the ones lost in the snow. Keeping your dog on leash while he is in booties makes it easier to know when to adjust them or to retrieve any that drop off.

A short-haired dog needs a winter sweater to stay warm.

2. Consider a wool or polypropylene sweater for a short-haired dog.

3. Encourage your dog to walk behind you in your tracks. It is less strenuous.

4. Take a small sled or snow disk with an insulated foam pad so your dog can rest off the frozen ground.

5. Keep your outings short in winter and carry snacks like liver or jerky treats and warm drinking water.

Spring, in some parts of the country, means heavy rain, mosquitoes, fleas, ticks, and a new crop of poison oak and poison ivy. Find out what you are in for so you can be prepared.

Fall announces hunting season in many parts of the backcountry. Check the hunting regulations and dates for the hiking area you have in mind. Most important, you and your dog should wear bright colors when hiking anywhere in the fall. Orange hunting vests are available for dogs, and colorful harnesses and bandannas are a good idea. When in doubt about hunting, keep your dog on a leash on forested trails.

Communicating with Your Dog

Your dog's two ways of communicating with you are through body language and vocal sounds. Listen to what he is trying to tell you by paying attention to his changes in demeanor on the trail. He is giving you important information about how he feels physically and his concerns about what awaits around the bend.

Body language: When everything is okay, your dog will have a light, relaxed sway and an energetic bounce in his step. Ears suddenly forward and tail up or raised hackles (hair standing up on the back of his neck or base of the tail) indicate tension and alertness triggered by a smell, sound, or sight.

Vocal communication: If your dog appears uneasy, hyperactive and alert and begins to bark, growl, or whine, she could be sensing a possible threat. The unusual smell, sound, or sight may not be visible to you, but respect her concern. Stop, listen, and look around. Pat your dog and speak to her reassuringly while keeping your wits about you. Make sure your dog is leashed and proceed cautiously until you identify the source of her concern, which can be as simple as another hiker around the bend or the presence of a rodent in the bushes.

Be sensitive: Tail down, stiff gait, and a lethargic pace may indicate a tightening of your dog's back or hip muscles from straining or bruising of soft tissue. Examine him carefully, checking his paws and between the toes for cuts or foreign bodies that could be causing him discomfort or pain. If he appears okay, stop and rest and make sure he gets water. He may need a snack to boost his energy.

If your dog looks drained, demoralized, or sick; is injured; or you cannot explain his odd behavior, trust that something is wrong. Dogs in general have an almost misplaced desire to please, even when in pain. Be considerate of your best friend's needs and limitations. Do not push him and jeopardize his well-being to meet your expectations and goals. On the trail you are a team and your teammate depends on you. Alter the route, and when in doubt cut the excursion short. In the unfortunate event that there is something serious going on with your dog, you may have to carry him out. You want to share safe, positive experiences that will nurture your enthusiasm for hiking.

On the other hand, fatigue at the end of the day is normal. A mellow dog after a solid day's work and play on the trail is a good thing. After a meal and a good night's rest, your dog should emerge refreshed in the morning. If he's dragging, take it easy by hiking a shorter distance to your next campsite or making extra rest stops on the way to the car if this is the end of the trip. (See Chapter 11 for suggested treatment of sore muscles.)

Preventive Care

Let your dog's pace determine the pace of the hike. Keep her on leash during the first thirty minutes of the hike. Off leash fresh out of the starting gate she may run around in a burst of energy and tucker herself out too soon because she has no way of knowing to pace herself.

Stop frequently for water breaks and use the stops to examine your dog from head to tail. Remove the packs and check for chafing. Run your hands along her body, feeling for foxtails and burrs before they become a problem. Check her feet for worn pads and foreign bodies lodged between the toes.

Foxtails

The arrowlike grasses are at their worst in late summer and early fall, when the grasses are dry, sharp, and just waiting to burrow in some dog's fuzzy coat. The dry foxtail can be inhaled by a dog, lodge itself in the ear canal or between the toes, and camouflage itself in the dog's undercoat, puncturing the skin and causing infection. Foxtails have the potential to cause damage to vital organs.

Inspect your dog's ears and toes and run your hands through his coat, inspecting under the belly, legs, and tail. Brush out his coat out after excursions where there were even hints of foxtails. Violent sneezing and snorting is an indication he may have inhaled a foxtail. Even if the sneezing or shaking decreases in intensity or frequency, the foxtail can still be tucked where it irritates only occasionally while it travels deeper, causing more serious damage. Take your dog to a vet as soon as possible. Your dog may have to be anesthetized to remove the foxtail.

Poison Ivy, Oak, and Sumac

These three-leaved, low-growing plants (poison oak has shiny leaves) can cause topical irritations on hairless areas of your dog's body. (You can apply cortisone cream to the affected area.) Find out if there is poison ivy (usually in the eastern states), poison oak (mainly in the western states), or poison sumac where you plan to hike, and make sure you wash your hands with soap after handling your dog. The resin can rub off your dog onto you, your sleeping bag, your car seat and your

Poison ivy

Poison oak

furniture at home. If you are very sensitive to these rashes, bathe your dog after the hike and sponge your arms and legs with diluted chlorine bleach or Tecnu soap, an outdoor cleanser that removes plant oil from your skin. Tecnu soap also can be used on your laundry.

Other Poisonous Plants

Unfortunately, your dog may be tempted to chew and taste hazardous plants. This includes plants found in your backyard, like rhubarb. In the wilderness, however, there are similar dangers—plants such as rhododendrons and Japanese yew may cause considerable sickness and discomfort for your pet. If you suspect poisoning, take note of what your dog ate and head back to the car. Once out of the woods, call your vet or an animal poison control center. (See Appendix C.)

Fleas and Ticks

Fleas are uncomfortable for your dog and carry tapeworm eggs, and ticks are one of nature's most painfully potent and tenacious creatures for their size. Some ticks cause uncomfortable, swollen irritation to the area of the skin where they attach or inflict temporary paralysis. Other types of ticks carry Rocky Mountain spotted fever and Lyme disease, the latter of which is reported to be the most common tick-carried disease in the United States.

Where Do Dogs Get Ticks?

Ticks thrive on wild hosts (deer are the most common) around lakes, streams, meadows, and some wooded areas. Ticks cling to the unsuspecting hiker or dog. On dogs, they crawl out of the fur and attach to the skin around the neck, face, ears, stomach, or any soft, fleshy cavity. They attach to their hosts by sticking their mouthparts into the skin to feed on the host's blood.

Removing a Tick

1. Try not to break off any mouthparts (remaining parts can cause infections), and avoid getting tick fluids on you through crushing or puncturing the tick.

2. Pinch tick at base of skin and twist as you pull it.

3. Grasp the tick as close to the skin as possible with blunt forceps, or tweezers, or with your fingers in rubber gloves, tissue, or any barrier to shield your skin from possible tick fluids.

4. Remove the tick with a steady pull.

5. After removing the tick, disinfect the skin with alcohol and wash your hands with soap and water.

There is an abundance of chemical and natural flea and tick products on the market, including collars, dips, sprays, powders, pills, and oils. Some products have the advantage of being effective on both fleas and ticks, remain effective on wet dogs, and require an easy once-a-month topical application. Consult your veterinarian about a safe and appropriate product.

Mosquitoes

Avon's Skin-So-Soft is a less toxic and more pleasant-smelling mosquito repellent, than—though not as effective as—repellents containing DEET. Mix one cap of the oil with one pint of water in a spray bottle. Spray your dog and run your hands through her coat from head to toe and tail to cover her with a light film of the mixture. Be careful to avoid her eyes and nostrils, but do not miss the outer ear areas. Orgainic solutions containing eucalyptus can be used as a mosquito repellent.

Besides being annoying, mosquitoes carry heartworm. Consult your veterinarian about preventive medication.

CHAPTER TEN

Wildlife Conflicts

Most hikers with dogs come to the natural world "in peace" to retreat and absorb the beauty. Nevertheless, you are still an uninvited guest at best. Respect the animals whose home you are in, and trespass lightly.

Protecting Wildlife

Leashes are mandatory in many outdoor recreation areas primarily to protect the wildlife that lives, breeds, migrates, or nests there. Even in areas where your dog is allowed off leash, do not let him chase wildlife or livestock for sport. It stresses and depletes the animal of survival energy and can cause a serious injury that leads to a cruel, agonizing death.

In the spring nesting birds are very vulnerable to free-roaming dogs in meadows and low brush. Young deer can be separated from their mothers and fall prey to your dog's primal but inappropriate impulses.

Your companion is more likely to chase wildlife at the beginning of the hike, when he is fresh out of the starting gate. Keep him on leash for about thirty minutes while he walks off some of his excess energy and gets used to his surroundings.

If you have any doubts about your dog's behavior, keep him leashed.

Preventing Encounters

The potential for being injured or killed by a wild animal is extremely low compared with many other natural hazards. Information and preparedness is the safest way for hikers with dogs to enjoy their time on the trail. Although there is no absolute rule to wild animal behavior, there is sufficient knowledge to trust some established guidelines. When given the opportunity, most wild animals are more than happy to avoid humans; unfortunately, people often feed wild animals because they look cute and cuddly. Once a wild animal gets a taste of human food, it becomes habituated to human food and will not forget that humans are a source of food. Wild animals that have grown accustomed to human food and garbage can become brazen, posing a threat to human safety. In bears, these bad "human-engendered" habits identify them as "problem" bears, which sadly leads to their eventual and inevitable destruction. If you love wild animals, respect them, admire them from a safe distance, and do not feed them.

Be informed about where you plan to hike and what lives there. Contact the region's fish and game, park, or forest headquarters. Keep your eyes open and learn to identify tracks, scat, and concealed kill sites. Keep your dog on a leash in questionable surroundings.

Bears and Bear Safety

Development encroaching on habitat and more hikers in remote wilderness areas have increased the bear's exposure to humans, their food, and their garbage. It is more important than ever to know how to minimize the risk of an encounter and what to do if one occurs.

There is no scientific evidence that dogs are "bear bait." But a loose dog in bear country runs more of a chance of surprising a bear and antagonizing it with barking and other antics. Even if your dog gets lucky and runs back to you unharmed, your problems are just beginning if the bear follows.

Bear facts

Bears can run, swim, and climb trees.

Bears have good vision, excellent hearing, and a superior sense of smell.

Bears are curious and attracted to food smells.

Bears can be out at any time of day but are most active in the coolness of dawn and dusk and after dark.

Bears and wild animals in general prefer anonymity. If they know you are out there, they will avoid your path.

Stay on the trail, where there are fewer chances of surprising a bear snacking in a berry patch. Make your presence known with noise that is distinctly manmade, such as talking, singing, or humming a tune. The slight jingle of a metal ID tag against the metal rabies tag acts like a bell on your dog's collar or harness and can help notify bears of your presence. A small bell on the dog collar and one on your belt, walking stick, or boot lace is a stronger statement in grizzly country.

When it comes to odor, in bear country the motto is "less is safer." Pack all food items (human and dog) and any other odorous items in airtight resealable bags. Dispose of all items with food smells in airtight bags, in bear-proof storage containers. Clean your dishes and pet bowls as quickly as possible so food smells do not float through the forest as a dinner invitation to the local bears. Some national forests and wilderness areas require that campers use plastic portable "bear-resistant food canisters." These canisters (some collapsible) are available for sale and rent at sporting good stores and some ranger stations.

If you see a bear in the distance, stop, stay calm, and don't run. Keep your dog close to your side on leash. You should feel awe rather than panic. Walk a wide upwind detour so the animal can get your scent, and make loud banging or clanging noises as you leave the area. If the bear is at closer range, the same principles apply while you keep your eye on the bear and back down the trail slowly if the terrain doesn't allow you to negotiate a detour.

Avoid sudden movements that could spook or provoke the bear. Be cool, slow, but deliberate as you make your retreat. (To learn more about hiking in bear country, refer to *Bear Aware*, by Bill Schneider [Guilford, CT: Falcon, 2004].)

Mountain Lions

There are fewer mountain lions than bears, and the mountain lion population is concentrated in the western United States and Canada. As with bears, development and human intrusion are at the core of the encounter problems.

- Keep your dog on leash on the trail.
- Keep your dog in the tent at night.
- Seeing doesn't mean attacking. If you come across a mountain lion, stay far enough away to give it the opportunity to avoid you.
- Do not approach or provoke the lion.

Mountain lion facts

Mountain lions are elusive, and preying on humans is uncharacteristic.

Mountain lions are most active at dawn and dusk and usually hunt at night.

They are solitary and secretive and require a vegetated habitat for camouflage while they stalk prey.

Their meal of choice is big game (deer, bighorn sheep, and elk). In the absence of game, however, they can make a meal of domestic livestock and small mammals.

They feed on what they kill. An unattended dog in camp is far more appetizing than his kibble.

- Walk away slowly and maintain eye contact. Running will stimulate the lion's predatory instinct to chase and hunt.
- Make yourself big by putting your arms above your head and waving them. Use your jacket or walking stick above your head to appear bigger. Do not bend down or make any motion that will make you look or sound like easy prey.
- Shout and make noise.
- If necessary, walking sticks can be weapons, as can rocks or anything you can get your hands on to fight back with. (For more information on hiking in mountain lion country, refer to *Mountain Lion Alert*, by Steven Torres [Falcon Publishing, 1997].)

Make yourself look bigger by putting your arms above your head.

Other Animals

Bobcats

Smaller than mountain lions, these wild cats are no threat to humans and would prefer climbing a tree over confronting your dog.

Wolves

Even if there were enough wolves that you might have the privilege of seeing one, they would still be less than interested in you. They pose no identifiable threat to hikers. The few that are left live and hunt in packs as their ancestors did, and they stay far away from humans.

Coyotes

In spite of their ability to survive persecution in healthier numbers than their wolf cousins, coyotes are not a threat on the trail. Hikers are more fortunate than some homeowners, though. In some neighborhoods of southern California and the Southwest, loss of habitat to housing developments has increased the incidence of unattended pets turning into a meal for a coyote.

Skunks and porcupines

Skunks and porcupines are primarily nocturnal and will fend off the curious with a spray or shot of barbed needles, respectively. It's a good idea to carry lemon juice concentrate and a pair of disposable latex gloves (available in hardware store paint departments) in your pack in case your dog gets sprayed by a skunk. A lemon juice rub and stream water rinse will tone down some of the fumes until you can give your pooch a full spa treatment—with de-skunk shampoo mix—at a pet wash location, groomer, veterinarian, or in your own backyard. (See Chapter 11 for directions on administering a de-skunk bath.) Always carry a couple of dog towels or old sheets in your car to wrap your dog and protect your upholstery. In a pinch, large plastic trash bags and duct tape come in handy to create a barrier between the seats and a damp, stinky dog.

A dog pierced by a mask of porcupine quills is a pitiful sight. Few dogs can withstand the pain of having barbed needles pulled out of their faces by inexperienced, nervous hands without any anesthetic. Take your dog to a vet as quickly as possible.

Snakes

Most dogs have an instinctive aversion to lizards and snakes. Dogs will bound away at the first sight, sound, or touch of a slither. Snake bites are usually a result of stepping on a snake unknowingly rather than conscious provocation. Most snake bites occur on the nose or front legs and can be lethal to a small or young dog. If taken to the vet quickly, larger adult dogs will survive most bites. Ask your veterinarian if the recently developed rattlesnake vaccine would benefit your dog. Ask your vet or local dog club about snake avoidance classes in your area. (See Chapter 11 for information on treating venomous bites.)

Most dogs avoid snakes.

Spiders

Most spider bites cause mild irritation and swelling, but in the case of black widow spiders, their venom can be more lethal than snake venom. Seek veterinary attention if your dog is bitten by a black widow spider. (See Chapter 11 for information on treating venomous bites.)

Bees, wasps, hornets, and yellow jackets

A leash is the best preventive measure to protect your dog from her own curiosity. Insect nests can be in trees or on the ground. (See Chapter 11 for information on treating insect bites.)

CHAPTER ELEVEN

Medical Emergencies and Treatment

Planning, a common-sense approach, and a leash will help prevent most mishaps on the trail. Keep your dog on leash when:

- Hiking in territory known for its higher concentration of specific hazards (bears, mountain lions, snakes, skunks)
- Crossing fast-moving streams
- Negotiating narrow mountainside trails
- Hiking in wind and snow (dogs can become disoriented and lose their way)
- If your dog gets into trouble, here are some basic first-aid treatments you can administer until you can get him to a vet.

Carry a basic first-aid kit for trail emergencies.

Bleeding from Cuts or Wounds

1. Remove any obvious foreign object.

2. Rinse the area with warm water or 3 percent hydrogen peroxide.

3. Cover the wound with clean gauze or cloth and apply firm, direct pressure over the wound for about ten minutes to allow clotting to occur and bleeding to stop.

4. Place a nonstick pad or gauze over the wound and bandage with gauze wraps (the stretchy, clingy type). For a paw wound, cover the bandaging with a bootie. (An old sock with duct tape on the bottom is a good bootie substitute. Use adhesive tape around the sock to prevent it from slipping off. Be careful not to strangle circulation.)

Frostbite

Frostbite is the freezing of a body part exposed to extreme cold. Tips of ears and pads are the most vulnerable.

1. Remove your dog from the cold.

2. Apply a warm compress to the affected area without friction or pressure.

Heatstroke

Heatstroke occurs when a dog's body temperature is rising rapidly above 104 degrees F and panting is ineffective to regulate temperature.

1. Get your dog out of the sun and begin reducing body temperature (no lower than 103 degrees F) by applying water-soaked towels on her head (to cool the brain), chest, abdomen, and feet.

2. Let your dog stand in a pond, lake, or stream while you gen-

tly pour water on her. Avoid icy water—it can chill her. Swabbing the footpads with alcohol will help.

Hypothermia

Hypothermia occurs when a dog's body temperature drops below 95 degrees F because of overexposure to cold weather.

1. Take the dog indoors or into a sheltered area where you can make a fire.
2. Wrap him in a blanket, towel, sleeping bag, your clothing, or whatever you have available.
3. Wrap him in warm towels or place warm water bottles in a towel next to him.
4. Hold him close to you for body heat.

Insect Bites

Bee stings and spider bites may cause itching, swelling, and hives. If the stinger is still present, scrape it off with your nail or tweezers at the base away from the point of entry. (Pressing the stinger or trying to pick it from the top can release more toxin.) Apply a cold compress to the area and spray it with a topical analgesic like Benadryl spray to relieve the itch and pain. As a precaution, carry an over-the-counter antihistamine (such as Benadryl) and ask your vet about the appropriate dosage before you leave, in case your dog has an extreme allergic reaction with excessive swelling.

Skunked

When your dog gets skunked, a potent, smelly cloud of spray burns his eyes and makes his mouth foam. The smell can make you gag, and contact with the spray on your dog's coat can give your skin a tingling, burning sensation. Apply de-skunking shampoo as soon as possible.

De-Skunking Shampoo Mix

1 quart hydrogen peroxide
¼ cup baking soda
1 tablespoon dishwashing detergent

Put on rubber gloves and thoroughly wet your dog, apply mixture, and let stand for fifteen minutes; rinse and repeat as needed.

Sore Muscles

1. Rest your dog.
2. Apply cold-water compresses to tight muscle areas to reduce inflammation.
3. Administer ascriptin-buffered aspirin (check with your vet on dosage for your dog's breed and weight).

Venomous Bites

1. Keep your dog calm (activity stimulates the absorption of venom).
2. Rinse the area with water, and transport your dog to the nearest vet.

Cardiopulmonary Resuscitation

Check with your veterinarian or local humane society for pet CPR classes.

CHAPTER TWELVE

Trail Etiquette

Trail etiquette boils down to good dog manners and reliability. Even in areas where a leash is not mandatory, control is. Dogs can be shot for harassing livestock and wildlife. Trail etiquette is especially important for maintaining good relations between those with and without dogs.

At one time or another, your dog may be a partner in a dominance dance with another dog. This occurs more frequently between males, especially intact males that reek of testosterone. Dogs well-versed in pack hierarchy know to stay out of an alpha dog's face or to assume the subordinate body language that stops the music.

Minimize Dog–Dog Conflicts

Neuter your male dog before one year of age or as soon as both testicles drop. Overt dominance may not appear until he is two years of age. Neutering reduces macho and roaming instincts. Be aware that testosterone levels take several months to decrease after neutering.

Spay your female. Breeding females can be instinctively more competitive around other females. A female in season should never be on the trail. She will create havoc and her mating instincts will override her flawless obedience record of accomplishment for sure.

A leashed dog can be overly protective. *Avoid stress* by making a detour around other hikers with dogs or stepping off the trail with your dog at a sit while the other hiker and dog walk by.

Do not panic at the hint of raised hackles and loud talk. Most of it is just posturing. If your dog is off leash, keep walking away from the other dog while encouraging your dog to come in your most enthusiastic voice and with the promise of a biscuit. If she complies, reward her with a "good dog" and the promised biscuit for positive reinforcement. Walking back toward the dogs screaming and interfering before they resolve their conflict can stoke the fires of a more serious brawl. If the squabble escalates into a dogfight, make sure you cover your arms and hands before trying to break it up. Pull the dogs by the tail, lift their hind legs off the ground, or throw water on them to distract them. As a last resort, you may have to throw sand or dirt in the eyes of the one with the grip to pry her away. One hiker who uses a cane as a hiking stick reports having broken up a dogfight or two by slipping the crook of his cane under the dog collar or harness to drag the thug away.

Do not give treats to other hikers' dogs. Competition for food and protection of territory are the root of most dogfights.

Zero Impact

As our exploding urban populations rush to retreat in the backcountry, our fragile and diminishing ecosystems are at greater risk of collapsing under the weight of our hiking boots. More people competing for the use of limited recreation areas leaves dog owners vulnerable to criticism. So . . .

• Pack out everything you pack in.

- Do not leave dog scat on the trail. Bury it away from the trail and surface water. Or, better yet, carry plastic bags for removal.
- Hike only where dogs are permitted and abide by the regulations posted.
- Stay on the trail and in designated campsites in heavily used or developed areas.
- Step lightly in more remote pristine areas.
- Do not let your dog chase wildlife.
- Do not let your dog charge other dogs or hikers, regardless of his harmless exuberance and friendly intentions. A leash is a great pacifier around people who may not be comfortable with dogs.
- Dogs can spook horses and pack stock, putting riders in a precarious situation. Step off the trail and wait with your dog at a sit position until the traffic has passed. Always

On the trail with your dog, yield to other hikers and wildlife.

leash your dog when passing other hikers, cyclists, horse-back riders, or anyone with whom you are sharing the trail.

- Don't let your dog bark at hikers, pack animals, wildlife, or the moon. It is intrusive to those who choose hiking as an escape to quiet and serenity.

- Some hikers have strong opinions about why dogs should not be allowed in the backcountry. Avoid debating the issue of "hiking with dogs" with other hikers. Be courteous and use this opportunity to influence other hikers positively by keeping your dog on his best backcountry behavior.

Happy Trails!

There is no better playground than the great outdoors, and no better playmate than your dog. Plan, prepare, and safely share your best moments on the trail with your dog. Remember to pack the snacks, water, leash, and good sense and trail manners. Take good care of your hiking companion and he or she will take care of you.

CHAPTER THIRTEEN

Hiking on Public Lands

The United States has an extensive network of public lands available for recreation. They are divided in categories by use and administered by different government agencies, from the regional to federal level. Following are general descriptions and distinctions within our public land system and examples of varying dog policy.

The National Park Service oversees several hundred parks, historic sites, monuments, and recreation areas. The Park Service's first priority is conservation. Dogs are required to be on leash or physically restrained at all times; they may be permitted in the paved developed outdoor areas (front-country) but are almost never permitted on the hiking trails (backcountry).

Some of the exceptions to the rule include Devil's Tower National Monument, Wyoming; Devil's Postpile National Monument, California; Shenandoah National Park, Virginia; and Acadia National Park, Maine. For specific information on dog policy at national parks, contact the individual park you plan to visit. General information is available from the National Park Service Public Inquiries Office, Room 7012, P.O. Box 37127,

Washington, DC 20013; (202) 208–4747; www.nps.gov.

National Recreation Areas provide a playground for a broad range of outdoor activities, with an emphasis on water sports. Many allow dogs on leash. *National lakeshores, rivers,* and *seashores* are three other categories within the National Park system, with varying dog policies.

Grasslands cover one quarter of the earth's surface. In the United States, the National Grasslands Agency works to restore and preserve one of our most productive and abused ecosystems. National grasslands permit wandering off trail, picking grasses and flowers, and collecting rocks. Dogs on leash or under voice control are welcome.

The Bureau of Land Management (BLM) is a multiple-use resource and leans toward dog-friendly regulations. The BLM's 270 million acres were once described as "the lands nobody wanted," but outdoor enthusiasts recognize the recreational value of the West's rugged BLM lands. The former Fort Ord in Monterey, California, is an exceptional gem recently added to the BLM's collection of dog-friendly nature playgrounds. For more information, contact individual state Bureau of Land Management offices or BLM Public Affairs, 1620 L Street NW, Suite 406, Washington, DC 20240; (202) 452–5125; www .blm.gov.

National Forests were conceived more than 100 years ago to combine use and conservation. The nearly 200 national forests are scattered from coast to coast and stretch from Alaska to Puerto Rico, providing the largest number of dog-compatible hiking trails. Dog regulations vary from leash to voice control. For more information, contact the USDA, attention: Recreation, 1400 Independence Avenue SW, Mailstop 1125, Washington, DC; www.recreation.gov. To purchase

national forest maps, call (928) 443–8285 or visit www.fs.fed
.us/recreation/nationalforest/.

State parks are not among the most dog-friendly hiking
grounds, but some, such as Custer State Park in South Dakota,
Carmel River State Beach in California, and Henry Cowell Red-
woods State Park, also in California, allow leashed dogs on
trails.

Preserves and reserves are primarily concerned with
preservation and conservation. In some preserves dog restrictions are seasonal, based on wildlife breeding and nesting
cycles. Others, such as Point Lobos State Reserve in Carmel,
California, prohibit dogs from even entering the park in vehi-
cles. Contact the regulatory agency for individual open spaces
for specific regulations.

County and regional parks sometimes offer expansive
grounds and provide excellent day hiking. Usage regulations
vary with each individual park, from "no dogs allowed" to
"dogs under voice control." Grazing cattle is a common deter-
mining factor in dog policy at these parks.

North of the border many Canadian provincial and
national parks allow leashed dogs on trails. For park information, contact the Canadian Tourism Board at www.travel
canada.ca.

Membership in the American Automobile Association
(AAA) gives you access to tour books and camp books (free of
charge) for every U.S. state and Canadian province. Each tour
book includes a list and map of national, state, and other
recreational areas, including a chart indicating which have hiking trails and allow pets on leash. Contact the American Automobile Association at 800–JOIN–AAA for the location of the
closest AAA office.

Checklists

Day Hike Checklist

☐ Flea and tick treatment application prior to hike.

☐ Bug repellent in sealed plastic bag.

☐ Health and vaccination certificate.

☐ Collar and bandanna or colorful harness with permanent and temporary ID tag and rabies tag.

☐ Leather leash or expandable leash.

☐ Plastic water containers full of water: thirty-two ounce bottle for half-day hike (under four hours) and two-quart bottle for longer hikes.

☐ Eight ounces of water per dog per hour or 3 miles of hiking, in addition to water for you, to be carried with you.

☐ Water purifier for full-day hikes.

☐ Snacks for you and your pet.

☐ Collapsible dish or resealable bag.

☐ Plastic bags for cleaning up after your dog.

☐ Sunscreen for tips of ears and nose.

☐ Booties for pooch and comfortable, sturdy, waterproof boots for you.

☐ Wire grooming brush to help remove stickers and foxtails

from your pet's coat at the end of the hike.

☐ Extra clothing (sweater or coat for thin-coated dog; sweater and windbreaker for you).

☐ Extra large, heavy-duty plastic garbage bags (good to sit on and make a handy poncho in the rain).

☐ Flyers for a lost dog.

☐ Pocketknife (Swiss Army-type knife that includes additional tools: fork, scissors, pliers, file).

☐ Flashlight and extra batteries.

☐ Matches or cigarette lighter and emergency fire starter.

☐ First-aid kit.

☐ Telephone number and address of closest veterinarian.

Navigational Tools Checklist

☐ Topographic map (help with trail location, topography of the landscape, and elevation changes).

☐ GPS (global positioning system), best used in conjunction with topographic maps.

☐ Compass (backup if your GPS batteries die).

Backpacking Checklist

All items on day hike checklist, plus the following:

Dog Necessities

☐ Extra leash or rope.

☐ Dog packs for pooch and backpack with internal frame for you.

☐ Doggie bedroll (foam sleeping pad).

☐ Dog's favorite chew toy.

- ☐ Dog food (number of days on the trail times three meals a day).
- ☐ Additional water in a two-quart bottle.
- ☐ Water purifier.
- ☐ Dog snacks (enough for six rest stops per hiking day).
- ☐ Collapsible food and water dish (resealable bags).
- ☐ Nylon tie-out line in camp (expandable leash can be extra leash and tie-out rope).

Human necessities

- ☐ Tent with rain fly (large enough for you and your dog to sleep inside).
- ☐ Clothing (raingear, gloves, fleece or knit hat, long pants, wicking top, fleece top, socks).
- ☐ Camp stove and fuel bottle.
- ☐ Iodine tablets (backup water purifier).
- ☐ Food (lightweight nutritious carbs and proteins—instant oatmeal, dried fruits and nuts, pasta, rice, canned tuna, dehydrated backpacking meals, tea bags, or cocoa packets.
- ☐ Extra garbage bags.
- ☐ Bear-proof food canisters.
- ☐ Pepper spray (if hiking in bear country).

First-aid Kit

- [ ] First aid book.

- [ ] Muzzle—the most loving dogs can snap and bite when in pain. Muzzles come in different styles and sizes to fit all dog nose shapes.

- [ ] Ascriptin (buffered aspirin)—older dogs in particular may be stiff and sore at the end of a hike or a backpacking excursion. Consult your vet on the appropriate dosage.

- [ ] Scissors (rounded tips) to trim hair around a wound.

- [ ] Hydrogen peroxide (3 percent) to disinfect surface abrasions and wounds.

- [ ] Antiseptic ointment.

- [ ] Gauze pads and gauze.

- [ ] Clingy and elastic bandages.

- [ ] Sock or bootie to protect a wounded foot.

- [ ] Duct tape to wrap around a sock used as a bootie.

- [ ] Tweezers to remove ticks, needles, or foreign objects in a wound.

- [ ] Styptic powder for bleeding.

- [ ] Rectal thermometer.

- [ ] Hydrocortisone spray to relieve plant rashes and stings.

- [ ] Lemon juice for a quick rinse if you dog is skunked; recipe for de-skunking shampoo mix.

- [ ] Your veterinarian's telephone number and the telephone number of the veterinary clinic closest to the trailhead.

- [ ] National Animal Poison Control Center phone number: 888–426–4435.

Sources for Dog Hiking Gear and Accessories

Mail-order Catalogs and Web Sites

Wolf Packs
(541) 482–7669
www.wolfpacks.com

Petsmart
P.O. Box 910
Brockport, NY 14420–0910
(800) 872–3773
www.petsmartccom

OurPet's Company
1300 East Street
Fairport Harbor, OH 44077
(440) 354–6500
www.our-pets.com

Expedition Outfitters
www.expeditionoutfittersonline.com

Ruff Wear
www.ruffwear.com

Recommended Reading and Resources

Books and Pamphlets

Best Hikes with Dogs Series
The Mountaineers Books

Can You Turn a Wolf into a Dog
Pat Tucker and Bruce Weide
Send $2.00 to Wild Sentry/Hybrid Booklet, P.O. Box 172,
Hamilton, MT 59840; or download a version from
www.nwf.org/wildlife/pdfs/canyouturnawolfintoadog.pdf
(pamphlet)

*Dog Parenting: How to Have an Outrageously Happy,
Well-Adjusted Canine*
Andrea Rains Waggener with Patti Schaefer, DVM
Adams Media Corporation

The Encyclopedia of the Dog
Bruce Fogle, DVM
Dorling Kindersley Publishing

*Field Guide to Dog First Aid—Emergency Care of the
Outdoor Dog*
Randy Acker, DVM
Wilderness Adventure Press
(pocket size)

How to Be Your Dog's Best Friend
The Monks of New Skete
Little, Brown Book Group

Obedience—A Simple Solutions Book
Bowtie Press
(other useful dog training titles are also available in the
Simple Solutions series)

The Power of Positive Training
Pat Miller
Wiley Publishing, Inc.

The Wolf Within
David Alderson
Howell Book House

Phone Numbers

ASPCA-National Animal Poison Control Center: (888) 426–4435
(tape the number inside your first-aid kit).

American Veterinary Association: (800) 248–2862;
www.AVMA.org.

Web Sites

For topographic maps, visit
www.maps.nationalgeographic.com/topo/.

For informative articles, studies, and health alerts, visit
www.workingdogs.com.

For information on hiking with dogs in your city, county, or
state, visit www.google.com. In the search box, type "hiking
club dogs" and the name of the city, county, or state.

About the Author

Linda Mullally is a freelance writer who divides her time at home between Carmel Valley and Mammoth, California. She was the first travel columnist for *Dog Fancy* magazine, sharing information about dog-friendly getaways domestically and abroad while giving readers safety tips and promoting responsible dog ownership. Dogs have always been part of her life, camping, hiking, backpacking, and mountain biking across North America. She educates dog owners through articles and lectures on the treatment and care of man's best friend.